Revelations

Live in the Moment
Live Like There is No Tomorrow

C.J. Marie

Dedicated to my greatest inspiration of all my son, grandchildren, family, and friends.

With love always,

C.J.

Books by C.J. Marie

Timeless Elegance

Resolutions

Revelations

Reflections

Words of Wisdom

Accents of a Women

Captured Thoughts

Afterthoughts of Yesterday

Legacy of Stable Dreams

Shadowed Love

Reflections of Time

Melody of Love

Days of Difference

Children's Stories:

Mi Primer Dia-Escolar

My First Day in Kindergarten

Chap Books:

Of Love and Sorrow

Fly With Your Dreams

Guides:

Tell Me What to Do

Pageant Tips

Table of Contents

Introduction

Revelations means exactly that. Through our experiences many feelings surface. Through these feelings can your inner-being be revealed?

My hope is that reflecting on quotes will ignite an emotion that can lead you to self-knowledge and learn about yourself. Realizing and understanding why you feel the way you do can bring you the peace you are searching for to live a purposeful life.

Remembering Yesterday

Our minds often create magical thoughts. At times when I read a book, my mind captures those fantasy places that I will never set foot in and streets I will never walk on; however, they live in the imagination of my mind. As I silently wonder about life and the solitude of my quietness, the loneliness of my surroundings allows my imagination to enjoy the sanctuary of my mind.

My make-believe world that lives within my daydreams shadowing the past in my yesteryear youth. The bittersweet feelings linger as I remember those who have left this life in hopes of meeting them again in heavens shining light.

Within my writings, I hope you can find a piece of yourself, to stop and feel yesterday's memories. All those we love live in our hearts. We will be the legacy we will leave our children and their children. Living life is feeling alive each day otherwise we are merely existing waiting for life to pass. The good old days are filled with wonder and are meant to be held in our hearts forever. We must not live in what was but rather live in the present with hopes of a better tomorrow. Life without hope is a life without nothing.

Remember, it is health that is real wealth,
not pieces of gold and silver
Health is Wealth

— C.J. Marie

Some of the things you are never told; the hardest part of growing older is losing the people you love

– Judy Hale

I am not impressed by your position, title, and money. I am impressed by how you treat others

If you focus on the hurt, you will continue to suffer. You focus on the lesson, you will continue to grow

– The Chose One

Rumors can make you dislike innocent people. Don't judge people from what others are saying about them. Be wise, get to know them for yourself, this forms your own opinion. The one talking to you may be the one you need to stay away from

To be rich is not what you have in your bank account but what you have in your heart

You didn't become selfish; you became harder to manipulate.
Don't confuse the two

A tongue has no bones,
but it is strong enough to break a heart,
so be careful with your words

If you want to lift yourself up, lift someone else

— Booker T. Washington

Sometimes the universe never plays fair
and sometimes it has a sense of humor

— C.J. Marie

The past cannot be changed, edited, or erased.
It can only be accepted.
What you learn from it gives you the power
to move on and do better

If you push me away I promise you,
you won't find me where you left me.
My heart is big, but not big enough to deal with people
who decide to love me when it's convenient for them

Memories remind us that nothing lasts forever

Sometimes the strongest among us
are the ones who smile through silent pain,
cry behind closed doors,
and fight battles no one knows about

The best revenge is always to just happily
move on and let Karma do the rest

Sometimes it takes one story to bring back
a thousand memories

The biggest mistake we make in life is thinking we have time

*Crowns aren't made of rhinestones,
they are made of discipline, determination,
and a hard to find alloy called courage*

Don't look back with regret, look forward with hope

*Sometimes I wish I could just rewind back to the old days
with my loved ones and press pause...
just for a little while*

*I know now, after 50 years, that the finding, losing,
forgetting, remembering, leaving, returning, never stops.
The whole way of life is about another chance,
and while we are alive, till the very end,
there is always another chance*

— Jeanette Winterson

The truth is that all the stuff here on earth
we work so hard to buy and accumulate
does not mean a thing.
At the end of the day people will be cleaning out our 'stuff',
the stuff we've accumulated in our life.
The only thing of value that remains are the memories
and what we deposit into others.
May we all learn to spend less time accumulating stuff
and more time making memories

Mom, I see it in your eyes.
You are not here anymore,
and I know you will never return to the way you were.
You are fading away, soon to be gone forever

– C.J. Marie

True love never hates back

My tattoo of you is a validation that I will have
the feeling of you all the days of my life

You are the music I listen to, you are my forever

We all have issues because we all have a story
and no matter how much work you've done on yourself,
we all snap back sometimes.
So be easy on yourself.
Growth is a dance, not a light switch

— John Kim

When you wake up in the morning be thankful
for another chance at life and be proud of yourself
for having the strength to continue moving forward
through life's difficulty journey

— Roger Lee

Life is too short to worry about what others think of you.
As long as you believe in yourself and you are doing
what makes you happy because that's what really matters

— Roger Lee

*Sometimes in relationships one door closes
but a window opens, and the breeze of hope enters to wonder*

I can only light the path, but you have to walk it

*To reach a destination you have to choose a direction,
to be everywhere is to reach no where*

*Sometimes not saying anything is the best answer,
you see, silence can never be misquoted*

*Good friends care for each other period.
Close friends understand each other.
But true friends stay forever.
Beyond wounds, beyond distance, beyond time*

*Do everything with a good heart and expect nothing in return
and you will never be disappointed*

— Barbara Lowe

*Let us come above to the splendor that is all around us
and see the beauty in ordinary things*

*Moments become memories and people become lessons.
That's life*

— Pastor Tendai Mpofer

*Life is too short to waste your time with people who don't
respect, appreciate, and value you*

*When we get to the end of our lives together,
the house we had and the cars we drove, t
he things we possessed won't matter.
What will matter is that I had you and you had me*

You will always be my forever

*Life is like a book. Some chapters are sad, some are happy,
and some are exciting. But if you never turn the page you will
never know what the next chapter holds*

*If we could spread love as quickly as we spread hate
and negativity, what an amazing world we would live in*

*When you arise in the morning,
think of what a precious privilege it is to be alive,
to breathe, to think, to enjoy, to love*

— Maureen Aurelius

Sometimes silence is more peaceful than having the last word

*You don't always need to tell your side of the story.
Time will*

*Sometimes you will never know the value of a moment
until it is a memory*

Choice not chance determines your destiny

Sometimes I touch the things you touched
when you were here.
I am looking for the echoes of your fingers

— Iain Thomas

The world suffers a lot.
Not because of the violence of bad people,
but because of the silence of good people

— Napoleon

They have money for war, but they can't feed the poor

— Tupac

Live in the Moment

Live in the moment is my motto, and I encourage everyone to adopt the same mindset. This moment is the only one we are certain to have. Tomorrow is promised to no one, and it's easy to see how life can change in an instant. Instead of focusing on what is lacking in our lives, we should spend time celebrating the beautiful blessings that surround us. We often get distracted by the things we don't have and overlook the wonderful things we do have. As human beings, we are prone to wanting more, and our cravings never stop.

Gratitude is the only way we can truly appreciate each day, and we need to recognize and be mindful of this. We should be aware of our life and everything we are feeling as we experience it. Stop and take time to feel your emotions; Being aware of them is key to developing your inner self. For instance, when I return home from shopping, I give thanks for a safe journey. When I'm with friends, I pause and appreciate how wonderful it is to be in their company. There are so many moments we allow to go unnoticed.

Life can be challenging at times, but there are also countless joyous moments to be had. Life is what you make of it. The decisions are yours, and you have the power to control the tapestry and color of your own life. No one else can live your life for you. You need to remove the blinders and eliminate the negativity that drains your hope and energy.

Living in the moment is just that, living fully in the present. The past has gone forever, and if you choose to dwell on it, you prevent yourself from moving forward, resulting in a mundane existence. Worrying about what could happen in the future is a waste of time and energy. All we have is now; Tomorrow will eventually become part of your past. The present is a gift we often take for granted, especially when our thoughts are filled with negativity.

Live your best life now. Feel the good things that life has to offer each day. Remember, the present is fleeting, and now is all we truly have.

Some Things that Bring Simple Joy

Bird singing

The fresh smell of chamomile

Your first sip of morning coffee

The good feeling of getting into bed at night

Feeling the warmth of a hot shower

Sipping hot soup on a cold winter's day

Going into cool refreshing water at a pool or beach on a hot summer day

Breathing normally after a bad cold

Looking in the mirror wearing a great outfit and thinking I got this

Completing a task and feeling good about it

Take the first bite from your favorite food

Finding something you lost

Looking at a sunrise or a sunset

Making someone smile

Helping others

Being kind

Feeling good about getting something you wanted

Feeling grateful when you're in a warm house and there is a snow-storm outside

Feeling good about what you have without wanting more

The Power of Imagination

I magination is the birth place of new ideas. It is a vision formed in the mind, creating emotions and connecting you to your aspirations. It serves as the visual picture you paint within your thoughts, carrying energy that the universe responds to in various ways. Imagination acts as a motivator, sparking ideas that can enhance your life and propel you towards your goals.

Sometimes, imagination allows you to envision yourself in the place you want to be, offering a magical escape from reality. Many of the most successful and influential people have harnessed the power of their imagination to turn their dreams into reality. Mental images take on a life of their own, and whether they are positive or negative, only you hold the full control over them.

The mind is an extraordinary tool. It can guide you down a path of growth and positivity or trap you in thoughts of resentment and hate. This is why being mindful of your thoughts is crucial. Every idea, feeling, and the motion is controlled by your mind, and your thoughts often stem from your emotions. Being aware of this connection is essential to shaping a fulfilling life.

However, imagination alone is not enough. What you visualize in your mind remains a mere dream unless action is taken to bring it to life. By combining imagination with effort and determination, you can transform your vision into reality and create a future that aligns with your desires.

*One day you will wake up
and there won't be any more time
to do the things you've always wanted.
Do it now*

— Paulo Coelho

*Time doesn't wait,
indecision will only let opportunities slip by.
Pick a path then walk confidently
with your heart behind every step*

— Zantamato

*We can't always choose the music life plays for us,
but we can choose how we dance to it*

◆

*May your day be full of magic
and may you not be too busy to see it*

◆

I am unequivocally luminous, striking, bright, and sparkling.
I have a warm halo of gratefulness around me

– C.J. Marie

Never let your bad days make you forget all your blessings

Love all, trust a few, not everything is real
and not everyone is true

I will wait until the timing is right when the stars are aligned
and you are ready for this love of mine.
Take your time, clear what is on your mind
because to me you are worth the fight

– V.M. Enriquez

Sometimes you don't need to hear their excuses
because their actions already spoke the truth

Silence is a time of self-reflection.
We reflect on who we were, look at who we are
and envision who we could be, all to become our best selves

Do not spoil what you have by desiring what you have not
but remember that what you now have was once among
the things you only hoped for

— Epicurus

Never let fear of striking out get in the way

— Babe Ruth

The worst day of my life was the last day of yours

◆

You can't create chaos in the lives of others
and expect peace to come to yours.
No matter what they did or how you feel,
causing hurt to others will never bring healing to you

— Morgan Richard Oliver

If you see someone falling behind, walk beside them.
If you see someone being ignored, find a way to include them,
always remind people of their worth,
one small act could mean the world to them

We understand death only after it has its hands
on someone we love

— Madame De Stael

My side of the story doesn't matter anymore.
Life happened, it hurt, I healed, but most importantly,
I learned who deserves a seat at my table
and who will never sit at it again

Experience is the hardest kind of teacher.
It gives you the test first and the lesson afterward

— Oscar Wilde

I learned that courage was not the absence of fear,
but the triumph over it.
The brave man is not he who does not feel afraid,
but he who conquers that fear

— Nelson Mandela

No amount of regret can change the past.
No amount of anxiety can change the future.
Any amount of gratitude will change the present

— Ann Voskamp

It's not what you say its how you say it
and that's what makes a difference
in how you make a person feel

— C.J. Marie

Forget the Past

While reading other author's writings, certain words stood out to me in a way that felt deeply personal. It is often said that the past is the past, yet how often do we find ourselves reflecting on it, consumed by emotion, regret, anger, and anxiety? We must work hard to put the past into perspective. The pain and joy we have experienced in the past, have shaped who we are today.

One word in particular stands out to me: indifference. Throughout my life, I have strived to embrace this 12-letter word. This doesn't mean that I don't care about my past; rather, it means that I've learned to place it where it belongs, behind me.

It is important to learn from the past, to respect it, and to own it, but then to move forward. Indifference in this sense, is the emotional detachment from what has already happened. You will always remember the past, but it is crucial not to get caught up in it. My goal is to help others understand their inner feelings, to move forward with love and peace, and to embrace themselves fully in the present.

Love Remains

I remember how life once was, and I see how it is now, how much has changed over the decades. I longed for the good old days, when life and the world around me seemed simpler, and freedom was without fear. So much has changed. Loved ones have passed, holidays have been more difficult, and age has brought on its own challenges. Sacrifices have been made, compromises reached, all for the ones we love. What lies ahead remains uncertain, with answers that seem to whisper in the wind. There are so many uncertainties, yet, love remains.

Just you and me, as it was always meant to be.

A Tree Grows in Astoria

There was a large, shady tree that cascaded over the green bench in front of my grandparent's 2 family house in Astoria, Queens N.Y.. The roots of this enormous tree had begun breaking up the sidewalk, but it remained a magnificent sight. Its massive trunk became a perfect hide and seek hideaway. As I played on the stoop, I would often gaze at the tree and wonder what would become of it. At just 10 years old, I was so impressed by how big and strong it was, so beautiful in its own natural way.

Trees add so much beauty to our world. They provide homes for the little birds and places where squirrels can scamper up their bark and branches. Trees also absorb carbon dioxide from the air, helping our environment. Over time, I grew to love that tree deeply.

One afternoon, as I was coming home from school, I saw a huge truck parked in front of my house. To my shock, I saw my beautiful tree being cut down and taken away. The only thing left was the stump. I couldn't believe it. My beloved Astoria tree had been reduced to nothing. It was likely necessary for safety reasons, but in a strange way, I couldn't help but feel a deep connection to that tree. For so many years, I had looked out the window of the second floor and seen its leaves almost brushing against the bricks of my grandparent's house.

Now, it was gone. There would never be another tree like that one. It would take 100 years for a new tree to grow to the size and strength that this one had. As I said goodbye to the tree that had graced the sidewalk there's so many decades, a deep emptiness and sadness washed over me. I sat on its stump, watching the rest of its being taken away, and the pain overshadowed me. Even today, when I visit that house, I miss that tree. A piece of natural beauty was taken, replaced by a small, young tree.

It will take 75 to 100 years before this new tree can even begin to tower over its surroundings. It seems everything comes to an end, even the old, memorable tree I loved so much in Astoria.

A Feather from Heaven

I speak to my mother often, even though she has passed away. Her clothes still wait to be sorted and donated. Though some time has passed, I find it difficult to let go of them. Yet, I take comfort in knowing that they are there, a tangible reminder of her presence.

One morning in late January, as I was doing laundry in my laundry room, I felt the energy of my mom around me. I had bent down to pick up the detergent, and as I turned to face the machine, there, right where I would normally put the detergent, lay a beautiful 3 inch white feather. It was in a place I would have to see it.

When I saw the feather, my stomach did a flip. There was no way it could have gotten there on its own. I felt it was a sign from my mom, a visit from an Angel. As I held the feather carefully in my hand, I placed it gently on my mom's clothes (which were nearby), and a deep sense of peace washed over me. I felt that my mom was truly at rest.

For me, this was a very real moment. The message was clear, and I gave thanks for this intervention. I will be forever grateful for this feather of revelation from heaven. Now, I believe my mom truly found the peace she was searching for all of her life.

Grief during the holidays can feel like we are living two lives.
One is where you pretend everything is okay,
surrounded by joy and festivities.
The other is where your heart silently screams in pain
missing what once was

When someone you love becomes a memory,
that memory becomes a treasure

When you give up on someone,
it's not because you don't care anymore,
it's because you realize they don't

Be like a butterfly, but sting like a bee

— Mohammed Ali

In a field of roses she is a wild flower

With no voice, you are invisible.
When your voice is heard, you become inspired

— C.J. Marie

Dance while you can because you never know
when the last dance will come

My Special Rocking Chair

I have a rocking chair that is one of my most priceless possessions. Purchased by my grandparents 50 years ago, this chair holds countless memories. I fed my child his bottles in it and rocked him to sleep when he needed extra comfort. Needless to say, wherever I go, my rocking chair will follow.

Today, it sits in my bedroom, where I enjoy my morning coffee, afternoon tea, and night time dessert. My rocking chair has given me endless pleasure and comfort over the years. I cherish the memories it holds.

My hope is that, in the years to come, this rocking chair will be passed down to my son, and then to my grandchildren. I hope they will value it as much as I do. I have been blessed to find a peaceful corner of my world where I can reflect on my memories with gratitude.

The Sweet Sorrow of Time

Another year has come and gone, and we are all feeling a little older. Last summer's heat was scorching hot, and winter's chill felt so much colder.

There was a time, not long ago, when life was full of fun and cheer. But now I truly understand, what it means to hold the past so dear.

We used to go to weddings, football games, and beaches and many other exciting events. Now we find ourselves more often at the funerals followed by brunches.

Dining out was once a treat, we would eat and laugh until we were full. Now we bring home half the meal, and chase it down with a mighty pill.

We used to travel far and wide, adventures crawling from near and far. Now we feel the aches and pains just from sitting too long in the car.

Nightclubs and a drink or two, were once the way we'd end the night. But now we stay at home instead and catch the news before it's light

And so my friend, this is life, a tale of growing old, you see. So cherish each day and live it well. Before your too darn old like me.

P.S. Yes I'm grateful for every year and thankful that I still can laugh. For every wrinkle tells a story and every laugh is a joyful draft.

Change

As I sit and reflect on the decades that have beautifully passed, I think of the changes that have transpired. So many loved ones have left us, and so many have been born along this journey of life. Friends and acquaintances have enriched our lives, all others we have chosen to forget.

As I look at old photos, a veil of sadness sometimes overshadows me. I am amazed at how time, and the loss of youth, have transformed me in so many ways. One thing is for certain you can't stop time. Mirrors and scales don't lie. Everyone has their own personal story to tell. We only need to get real and ditch denial. Keep in mind that, no matter how great you may look, age is still there.

Celebrate your age. Be proud of it. The winter of our lives is a challenge, but life is a learning experience filled with highs and lows, twists and turns, and the aches and pains that come with it. Still, we must remind ourselves of the blessings that surround us.

Embrace the future chapters of life, and believe that your purpose here on earth has touched many lives. Live with a peaceful heart.

Poison

Poison is lethal, and negative thoughts can be just as harmful. Suppressed anger often gives way to depression, and over time, anger turns into hate. Hate, in turn, poisons the soul. It leads only to disconnection, isolation, and the darkness that overshadows life. It is the minds destructive machine, mixing a poisonous potion that harms humanity. This evil, conjured up in the minds of the corrupt, poisons not only individuals but society as a whole.

Those who lack conscious are the true mental problems in our society. I often wonder how they arrived at such a state of mind. What events or circumstances in their lives led them to this point of disconnection from humanity? Now, more than ever, I find myself questioning and fearing the world around us. Why has humanity become so ugly?

Evil is among us, and somehow, we must combat it with good. The devil works in every aspect of life, spreading poison wherever it can. We must be vigilant and beware of the evil that surrounds us.

English Proverbs

Time flies; Time passes quickly

Old is gold; Old is valuable

A fool's paradise; False happiness

Silence is golden; Quiet is wise

Better safe than sorry; Be cautious

Honesty is the best policy; Truth wins

Look before you leap; Think first

Too little, too late; Help came too late

Walls have echoes; Be careful with secrets

Patience is a virtue; Waiting is good

No pain, no gain; Hard work pays

The last straw; Final breaking point

Birds of a feather, flock together

Patience pays off; Waiting yields results

Laughter is the best medicine; Joy heals

Knowledge is power; Learning is strength

Don't cry wolf; Don't give a fake story

Keep your powder dry; Stay prepared

No man is an island; We all need others

Make the most of today; Live in the moment

Author's Note

In this, my second book in the **Trilogy of Timeless Wisdom** series, my goal is to uncover the truth about your inner self. By removing the veil of denial and exploring your authentic truth, you can move toward peace and understanding. Through reflection and self observation, we can live the lives we are truly meant to live.

The Trilogy of Timeless Wisdom

by C.J. Marie

Each of us carries stories, lessons, and moments that shape who we become. Through *Reflections, Revelations,* and *Resolutions,* C.J. Marie invites readers on a heartfelt journey toward self-discovery, gratitude, and renewal.

Together, these three volumes form **The Trilogy of Timeless Wisdom** – a celebration of life's beauty, faith, and resilience. Each book stands alone as a companion for the soul, yet together they form a complete portrait of inspiration that uplifts the heart and quiets the spirit.

"Discover the words that endure. The lessons that uplift. The wisdom that never fades."

**Collect all three in
The Trilogy of Timeless Wisdom:**
Reflections • Revelations • Resolutions
– available wherever inspiring books are found –

About the Author

C.J. is the author of many inspirational books. An educator by profession, she has received numerous awards for her writing achievements. She is featured in Who's Who Among American Teachers and, as an entrepreneur, she was honored with the International and Business Career Award, C.J. has been recognized by the New York Assembly with a "Woman of Distinction" citation, as well as being selected as one of The Empowered Women of Queens, New York.

C.J. is a certified life coach and a personal consultant specializing in pageantry. As a multi-time, state and national queen, herself, she understands the importance of style and fostering a positive self-image. With over forty years of experience in the pageant arena, C.J. brings a wealth of knowledge and expertise to her work.

Beyond her professional accomplishments, C.J. is deeply involved in her community. She participates in bereavement groups, offering support to those dealing with grief. As a philanthropist, she devotes her time, talents, and resources to various charitable causes. Her artwork has been used to raise funds for churches and events, and she has donated proceeds from her book sales to those in need.

C.J's mission is rooted in service, bringing smiles, hope, and joy to those who need it most. She firmly believes that life's greatest rewards come from giving to others. For her, the most meaningful accomplishments transcend financial success and lie in the positive impact made on the lives of others.

www.ingramcontent.com/pod-product-compliance
Lightning Source LLC
Chambersburg PA
CBHW050908120626
46554CB00003B/1078